DATE DUE 7502188

WITHDRAWN

PENGUINS
LIVE HERE

Other books by *Irmengarde Eberle*

PENGUINS LIVE HERE

BY
IRMENGARDE EBERLE

Doubleday & Company, Inc.
GARDEN CITY, NEW YORK
1974

Alfred M. Bailey from National Audubon Society, 21
Stanley N. Botwinik from National Audubon Society, 7, 11
Philip Gendreau from National Audubon Society, 33
Olin Sewall Pettingill, Jr., from National Audubon Society, vi, 15
Michael C. T. Smith from National Audubon Society, 19, 25, 27, 29, 37
United Press International Photo, 5, 13, 17, 35
Wide World Photos, 3, 9, 23, 31

Library of Congress Cataloging in Publication Data
Eberle, Irmengarde, 1898–
    Penguins live here.
    SUMMARY: A brief description of the physical
characteristics and habits of the Adélie penguins of
Antarctica.
    1. Adélie penguin—Juvenile literature.
[1. Adélie penguin. 2. Penguins.] I. Title.
QL696.S473E23   1975   598.4'41
ISBN 0-385-05437-8 Trade
ISBN 0-385-05715-6 Prebound
Library of Congress Catalog Card Number 74–1383

PENGUINS
LIVE HERE

A group of Adélie penguins was swimming in the cold antarctic sea. They had been far down toward the South Pole. The water was their home, their main world.

It had been many months since they had come out to stand on bare rocks—rocks not covered with ice and snow. Now, when it was early autumn in that region, the need to go back to such a place lay in them like a strong memory.

They kept busy hunting for small fish to eat—herring and several other kinds. In their search they sometimes swam under shelf ice, extending from frozen white shores. And again they hunted out in the open sea.

They were sea birds, but they never stayed on top of the water like ducks. They spent most of their time underwater. Every once in a while they had to come to the surface for air. But they stuck out only their heads. Quickly they breathed in air for their bodies' immediate needs, and they gulped enough more to fill the air sacks in their short thick necks, in bones under the skin, and throughout their bodies. Then down they dived again into their watery world. It was those air pockets that made it possible for them to stay below such a long time.

Though there was still much open water at this time of the year, the nearby land lay deep under ice and snow, hard packed from thousands of seasons of polar winters and summers.

The penguins in the water stayed in a loose crowd and did most things together. There was always a leader, but every once in a while the leader dropped behind to let another take charge.

When one of them saw a school of small fish to one side or straight ahead, his sudden movement toward them was a signal to the other penguins. Immediately all turned the way the leader was going. And soon all were snapping up fish with their brick-red beaks and swallowing them as fast as they could.

Sometimes when they wanted to land, they came to the surface beside a silent, frozen coast, with cliffs dropping down to the sea. There they could not climb up. They took in a new supply of air and swam on to a place where the snow and ice sloped more gently. Then some of them came out on the icy shore, and after preening themselves to get rid of the water and ice on their feathers, they stood erect on their short legs and rosy, webbed feet, gazing out to sea. They looked like little concert conductors about thirty inches tall, in fine white shirts and black coats. They had wings, but these were not for flying. The feathers on the wings were scalelike. Actually they were like flippers and they used them entirely for swimming.

The penguins could shoot up fairly steep banks—four to five feet high, but not ten or twenty feet straight up, like some ice cliffs. When they were far under shelf ice, they sometimes came upon a hole in it and shot themselves straight up through it. They had remarkable strength for this upward and forward thrust. It was as though small, strong engines propelled them.

This group of about forty had been fishing steadily for many months. But the urge to go to their nesting areas was growing stronger, and abruptly they turned that way and darted forward again.

In some places they saw ice floes overhead on top of the water. These were in the in-between waters where it was slightly less cold. These flat, floating pieces of ice had broken off of the ice shelf that extended out from the continental coast.

They decided to land for a little rest beside a floe. As they came out of the water and stood on the large floating ice island, they saw that other Adélie penguins were already there—hundreds of them. These were making all their familiar noises in communicating with each other. As our group stared at them, the strangers began a march down to the sea. Soon they were swimming away. It was the season when all Adélie penguins go to their nesting areas—hundreds of thousands of them from here and elsewhere.

Our small group watched for a while, then they too slipped off the ice and into the ocean again. They too shot forward, well underwater, following their instincts. Soon—and for several months to come—the penguins would take on an entirely different life style from their almost continual swimming in the water.

They felt best in very cold water, but none the less this journey to milder air and bare rocks had to be made. They swam for many more days. Once when they surfaced, they saw a rocky island. But it did not suit them. They stayed here only a while, then left. There was only one island—a special island—for which they aimed.

Among the penguins there was a male, about six years old. He swam vigorously with the rest, yet he took time to look about a little for his mate.

He and his mate had nested together last year and the two years before that. During the winter months

8

he had often seen her. Sometimes he had stood on a frozen coast with her, and they had touched beaks and walked about or stood beside each other. At that time there had been no need to stay together continually. And their fishing expeditions often kept them apart within the group. Now the male was aware of a greater need for her. But he did not see her among those close around him.

The penguins swam without fear, as they were accustomed to the sea. They saw many sea creatures as they went along.

One day they saw several humpbacked whales that looked worse than they were. The penguins swam in a great curve around them. These whales ignored them, though some will eat penguins—especially the dangerous killer whales.

There was another enemy—the leopard seal. This kind of seal usually caught penguins in the water, seldom on ice-covered land or on rocks. But he always landed to eat his catch. One day on the journey the lead penguin saw one of these seals coming toward them underwater. The rest of the penguins got the signal, and in a few moments the whole crowd had scattered in all directions. But the seal caught one and carried her off to eat on shore. After a while the rest of the penguins came together again. The disturbance among them died down, and they darted on.

Finally they came to the island they were seeking—

an island close to the shore of the antarctic continent. To them this place was like no other. A part of it had been theirs for many years. All of this group had been hatched here, and all nested here. It was late afternoon when they saw the place.

On reaching the first rocks, the lead penguin quickly shot up on shore. He shook himself and stripped the water from his feathers with his beak. Then he stood erect and watched his companions until the last and slowest was safely up on the rocks. And now many males and females, mates for life, found each other. Most gabbled among each other for a few minutes. But not our male penguin who had been looking for his mate for so long. He stood aside, alone.

If she did not come, what would he do?

Now all penguins of his group seemed to be ashore. The whole crowd began to move away to seek their own personal nesting places of seasons past. Our male penguin, still seeking his mate, made complaining wails and then went with the others. He passed many piles of nesting stones and saw their owners claim them. Finally he came to his own nest. He had found it as easily as though it had been marked with a sign for him.

He stood beside it, still waiting for his mate.

But she did not come. Perhaps it was she who had been killed by the leopard seal in the ocean.

But no. All of a sudden she came up from the rear of the settling Adélie penguins. Her mate saw her and gave an excited welcoming squawk. When she was near him, they both turned their heads from left to right and right to left as though in a sign language. They made low sounds at each other. Then they came nearer and touched beaks and stood with their chests against each other. And he stroked her with his flippers. For the night, they stayed on their heap of rocks, sleeping where they stood. A few days later they mated.

Then they began to look their nest over more carefully. Like all the Adélie penguins' nests, it was made only of a pile of stones they had gathered the past year and years before. Looking at theirs now, they saw that it needed building up, so each went off to look for more stones. When they returned, they had small rocks in their beaks. They placed these on top of their old stone pile and went off again for more. They had to go quite a distance sometimes, for all the other penguins were looking for good stones too; and the nearby ones in the colony had already been taken.

After a while they had found enough so that the female stayed and arranged the stones to make a better nest. Now she was more choosy. Sometimes she would not accept the stone her mate brought. Then he

walked away as though not knowing what to do with it and finally left it lying somewhere.

These penguins were not the only ones on the island. Several other groups of Adélies had colonies nearby but separate. And farther away there was a colony of another kind. All together the various penguins in their colonies made up what men call a rookery.

There are a number of slightly differing species of penguins in the far southern regions of the world and in the antarctic. Some at times go as far north as the southern coasts of New Zealand and Australia and the Galápagos Islands. The Adélies stay farther south, where it is exceptionally cold.

Adélies are much bigger than the Fairy penguins of Australian coasts that measure only ten inches or so. Nevertheless they are shorter than the big, more important-looking King and Emperor penguins.

The stone nests of the Adélies are far different from the burrows that some of the other penguins make for hatching their eggs. Their customs in this come at least partly from necessity. There is no soil on their rocky islands. So there are no grasses or other low plants for nest building where the Adélies breed. And they are so accustomed to the intense cold farther south that even in nesting season they don't go too far north but stay quite naturally where it is not too warm for them. Even here, on this barren rock where our group settled, the mild weather sometimes made them open their beaks and pant.

Our penguin pair worked at their nest for several days. They had rounded out a small hollow at the top of the pile so that it was a little like the inside of a rough bowl.

All around them, only two to three feet away, the nests of the other penguins of their group were being repaired by their owners. The stone piles were so close together that the spaces between them were like little narrow valleys. The penguins could hardly walk between them without setting foot on a neighbor's pile. Mostly they managed to stay on their own heaps. But whenever one of them trespassed on another's, there was a quick squawk from the owner and sometimes a brief pecking fight. Then each went about his own business again.

Our penguin pair finished their nest, and the female sat on it. Only a few days apart, she laid two chalky white eggs. Then she got off the nest, and the male, who had been keeping her company nearby, came and stared at the eggs. Two eggs—that was right. There could have been three, but two were more usual. These eggs were important.

Now the female had done her part for the time being, so with a few satisfied squawks, she went off down to the sea to hunt for fish to eat and to give herself a sort of holiday.

The male climbed solemnly up on the rock pile and started incubating the eggs. He tucked them into the skin flap underneath his body, between his legs. The

18

flap was lined with thick, soft down, and here, next to his body, he could keep them evenly warm.

Overhead, as he sat there, sea birds flew and screamed their various notes. Some of these birds were dangerous, and our male penguin looked up at them guardedly now and then when they flew too low over him.

For a few days he sat all alone, doing the incubating, while inside the eggs the small new penguins were slowly beginning to form. Then his mate came back from the ocean. She preened herself, and when she was neat and dry she approached the nest. Again she and the male made low talkative sounds at each other. Then he arose and gently scraped the precious eggs out from under his skin flap with one of his webbed feet and his beak. Now she took her turn on the nest while he went off for his period of resting, swimming, and fishing.

Overhead, as the female now warmed and protected the eggs, the sea birds still circled. Among them were the dangerous Skua gulls—big brownish birds with a wide wingspread.

One day when the mother had to leave the nest briefly, a Skua dropped swiftly down, broke the eggs, and ate them. The female penguin ran at the Skua. She cawed and squawked in a furious clamor and pecked the robber bird.

All the other nesting penguins nearby looked nervously toward her and the enemy. Some of them came

20

and helped her attack the Skua. But they were not able to hurt him much. In any case, the two eggs were already lost. There was more wailing and squawking. The Skua finally flew off to look for more such unguarded eggs. Our female penguin stood bereft and waited for her mate. When he came it was evening. And seeing what had happened, he was as upset as she.

But in the next days they mated again, and soon the female laid two more of her fine, chalk-white eggs. This time she and her mate had better luck. No harm came to these eggs. The sea washed the rocky shore of the island. The sunshine was warm and bright most of the time. Comfortably cold winds blew now and then.

The enemy birds still flew overhead. So the weeks passed. Then one morning the eggs began to stir. The germs of life in them had grown into baby penguins, and they were about to hatch.

The male was on the nest when it began. He had just pushed one egg out of his flap to turn it over with his beak, and the next moment the egg cracked open on one side. He put his head down, every now and then, to watch. It took twenty hours from the first chip until the little one came out of its shell.

The female then sat on the nest and the father went off to catch food for his young one.

There was a pause of several days in which the female sat on the nest and warmed her first chick and continued to incubate the second egg. In three days the second chick hatched. The new one's damp down soon dried out in the body heat of the parent, and it joined its already fluffy brother in pleading for food.

Now again the parents took turns. One watched over the young and kept them warm and safe while the other went to sea for food. The hungry young ones ate all that the parents could bring. Father, and then mother, brought fish barely swallowed. And, opening

their beaks, they let the young ones take the food from inside their throats. When the chicks were big enough to be left alone, without too much danger, for a few hours, both parents worked to get food enough for them.

Once when the father came back from the sea with his catch, he was so top-heavy with the fish in him that he toppled over. The nearby penguins squawked and scolded. They were upset about him and did not stop fussing until he had righted himself and was safely walking on toward his young ones.

For weeks the parents kept on fishing for their chicks. Back and forth they went between the sea and the nest. And so they kept their young ones well fed, so that they grew fast—and strong and healthy. Then came a time when the chicks were almost as big as their parents, but still downy. Finally they molted and grew real feathers over their bodies and scaly feathers on their wings, like their parents. Before long they went to the sea with the adults and began to learn to swim, to catch fish for themselves, and to watch for dangers. Here too they met the young of other Adélie penguins and often formed groups with them.

When it was spring in the antarctic, the parents, with their young, joined the others of their colony down on the rocky shore. When all had gathered, they slipped into the sea and made their way back to the colder regions—even to the regions of perpetual ice. Every day other colonies from all over the island left too.

On their way southward, our penguins passed Gentoo penguins out fishing; and much later, on ice-covered land, Emperor penguins stood as though to greet them. They did not stop to join either of these groups. Farther and farther southward they went. The chillier waters were just right for the adults and the young ones were learning to live in greater coldness, too.

Once there was a spring snowstorm with high winds that raised wild waves. The Adélie penguins hardly noticed it as they were far under the surface of the water where it was quite calm.

At last they came to familiar regions—the land that lay so thickly covered with ice and snow the year round, in some places hundreds, even thousands, of feet deep. Here, as before, they often went ashore for a while. Once they were struck by a blizzard while they were on shore, so they gathered close together packed into a firm mass, all standing erect. The outer ones stood with their thickly feathered backs to the outside. And after a while others from inside changed places with them. This way none got too much of the bitterest cold.

The farther south they went the colder it grew, even though it was not now the coldest season of the year. Penguins young and old took it in their stride.

Many decades ago the early great European and American discoverers had come to the antarctic continent. Among them were the British explorers, Sir James Ross and, later, Sir Ernest Shackleford, and Admiral Richard Byrd from the United States. Others came from other lands. When they anchored their ships along a frozen coast, they saw penguins walking about and standing erect as though to greet them. And some penguins, full of curiosity, had gone quite close up to the ships and the men, expecting no danger from them.

The discoverers had been amazed to find these big birds so far south in the intense cold of the south polar regions. They were also surprised at their friendliness.

Explorers often saw these remarkable and handsome birds alone, in pairs or small groups, and sometimes hundreds of thousands of them gathered together.

Some of the antarctic explorers brought sled dogs to use for their work. These immediately became dangerous enemies of the penguins. For the dogs hungered to catch and eat them.

The sled dogs had been brought down all the way from the north polar regions. They too were used to the cold and could lie in the snow during a blizzard and sleep.

Later on, people who wanted to study penguins and their ways caught some, put them in cages, and took them to zoos in their own and other countries.

Fortunately men and their dogs have always been rather few in the intensely cold south polar regions. For life for human beings is most difficult there. Without the proper supplies, special clothing, and the know-how of protecting themselves, they cannot survive at all in the antarctic cold where the penguins are so comfortably at home.

Because so few men come there, most of the Adélies are not troubled by them or their dogs. They live quite peacefully in their groups, walking in their toddling way on the hard-packed ice and snow of the land, swimming weeks on end, and catching fish in the sea and bays of the cold, cold antarctic.

36

Irmengarde Eberle is the author of sixty-three books for children—highly regarded by librarians and people in general. A number have been Junior Literary Guild selections. Others have won awards, and some are published abroad in twenty-seven languages. She was born and brought up in Texas, and on graduation from college came east. She and her husband, Arnold W. Koehler, live in New York City.